BASIC/NOT BORING

SOCIAL STUDIES

Grades 2-3

Inventive Exercises to Sharpen Skills and Raise Achievement

Series Concept & Development
by Imogene Forte & Marjorie Frank
Exercises by Marjorie Frank

Incentive Publications, Inc.
Nashville, Tennessee

Thanks to Maurine Bridges for her assistance

About the cover:
Bound resist, or tie dye, is the most ancient known method of
fabric surface design. The brilliance of the basic tie dye design
on this cover reflects the possibilities that emerge from the
mastery of basic skills.

Illustrated by Kathleen Bullock
Cover art by Mary Patricia Deprez, dba Tye Dye Mary®
Cover design by Marta Drayton, Joe Shibley, and W. Paul Nance
Edited by Anna Quinn

ISBN 0-86530-396-7

PRINTED IN THE UNITED STATES OF AMERICA

TABLE OF CONTENTS

Appendix

CELEBRATE BASIC SOCIAL STUDIES SKILLS

Basic does not mean boring! There is certainly nothing dull about . . .

   . . . checking out the lumps and bumps on the Earth's surface

   . . . roaming all across North and Central America to gather stuff for a party

   . . . reading headlines from the past and creating headlines for the present

   . . . learning enough about government and traditions to design your own fantasy country

   . . . getting to know the dogs of Europe

   . . . finding out which state had the first pizza, the highest bridge, or has the most wild horses

   . . . discovering what eagles, bells, and fireworks have in common

These are just some of the adventures students can explore as they celebrate basic social studies skills. The idea of celebrating the basics is just what it sounds like—enjoying and improving skills that help you learn about people, their places in the world, and their activities. Each page of this book invites young learners to try a high-interest, visually appealing exercise that will sharpen one specific social studies skill or concept. This is not just an ordinary fill-in-the-blanks way to learn. These exercises are fun and surprising. Students will do the useful work of sharpening social studies skills while they follow two inquisitive children and their pets around the community, country, and world. Along with these fictional characters, they can learn about how people live together, grow, work, and learn in the world.

The pages in this book can be used in many ways:
- to review or practice a skill with one student
- to sharpen the skill with a small or large group
- to start off a lesson on a particular skill
- to assess how well a student has mastered a skill

Each page has directions that are written simply. An adult should be available to help students read the information on the page. Students should also have maps and other social studies resources available. In most cases, the pages will be used best as a follow-up to a lesson that has already been taught. The pages are excellent tools for immediate reinforcement of a skill or concept.

As your students take on the challenges of these adventures with social studies, they will grow! And as you watch them check off the basic skills they've strengthened, you can celebrate with them.

The Skills Test

Use the skills test beginning on page 58 as a pretest and/or a post-test. This will help you check the students' mastery of basic social studies skills and will prepare them for success on achievement tests.

SKILLS CHECKLIST
SOCIAL STUDIES, GRADES 2-3

✔	SKILL	PAGE(S)
	Locate own home in the universe	10, 11
	Examine and define neighborhoods	10, 11
	Use a map of a neighborhood	10, 11
	Use map skills to locate places and find information on maps	10–13, 28–37, 54–56
	Identify and find places in a community	12, 13
	Identify and describe services in the community	12, 13, 17, 18
	Identify different kinds of transportation and their uses	14
	Recognize signs found in the community	15
	Recognize some features of local government	16, 17
	Identify current officials of local and federal governments	16, 44
	Identify some ways local taxes may be spent	17
	Differentiate between rules and laws	19
	Recognize that people follow customs; define custom	20
	Differentiate between needs and wants	21
	Identify some kinds of jobs in the community	22, 23
	Differentiate between goods and services	23
	Explore concepts of managing and using money	24, 25
	Identify products and resources	26, 27
	Determine the resources used to make a product	26, 27
	Recognize some U.S. states	28–33
	Locate and name some states and cities in the U.S.	28, 29
	Locate own city, state, and country on maps	28, 29, 33
	Make a map of your state, locating your town and other key features	33
	Recognize and locate some countries that are neighbors to the U.S.	34, 35
	Identify landforms on a map	36
	Locate countries, regions, oceans, and continents on a map or globe	37
	Locate some features and landmarks around the world	38
	Differentiate between cities, states, countries, and continents	39
	Recognize some characteristics of different cultures	40–43
	Become familiar with some names and locations of countries	40–43
	Identify the three branches of government in the United States	44
	Identify and describe important American traditions, symbols, and holidays	45
	Explore traditions & symbols	46, 47
	Recognize & describe the American flag	48
	Identify key events in U.S. history	49, 50
	Read a timeline of historical events	49
	Identify some current events in own town or city	51
	Identify some important Americans and their accomplishments	52
	Describe some responsibilities of citizens	53
	Find information on a population chart	57

SOCIAL STUDIES
Grades 2-3

Skills Exercises

What's New in the Neighborhood?

A **neighborhood** is a place where people live. Every neighborhood has homes. The homes in this neighborhood are very close together.

There's a new kid in the neighborhood! Help Abby find her way around.

Use the map to answer the questions about her new neighborhood.

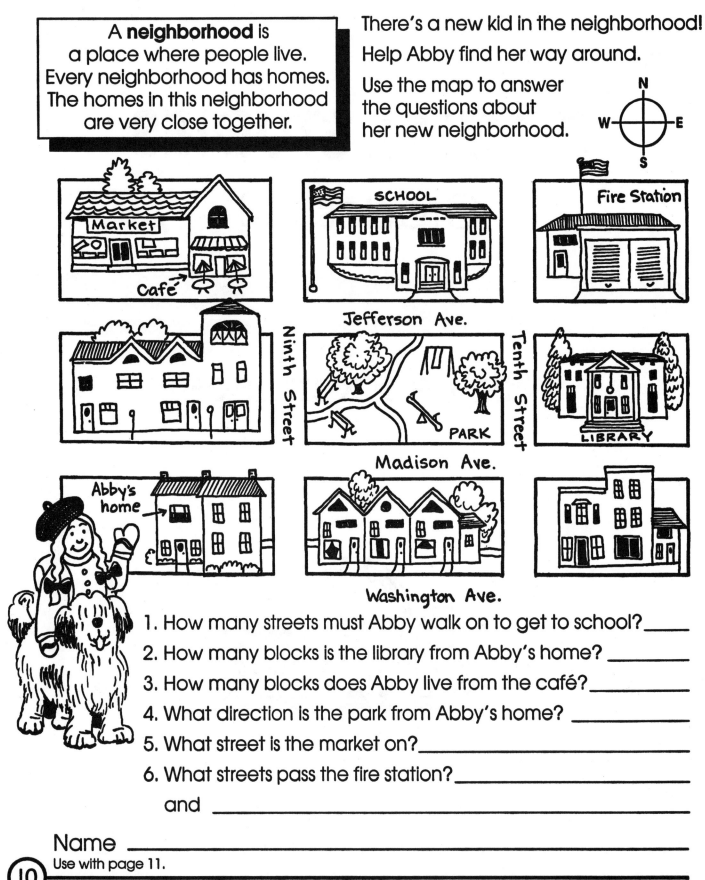

1. How many streets must Abby walk on to get to school?_____

2. How many blocks is the library from Abby's home? _____

3. How many blocks does Abby live from the café?_____

4. What direction is the park from Abby's home? _____

5. What street is the market on?_____

6. What streets pass the fire station?_____

   and _____

Name _____

What's New in the Neighborhood? cont.

There's a new kid in this neighborhood, too!

Help Mario find his way around.

Use the map to answer the questions about his new neighborhood.

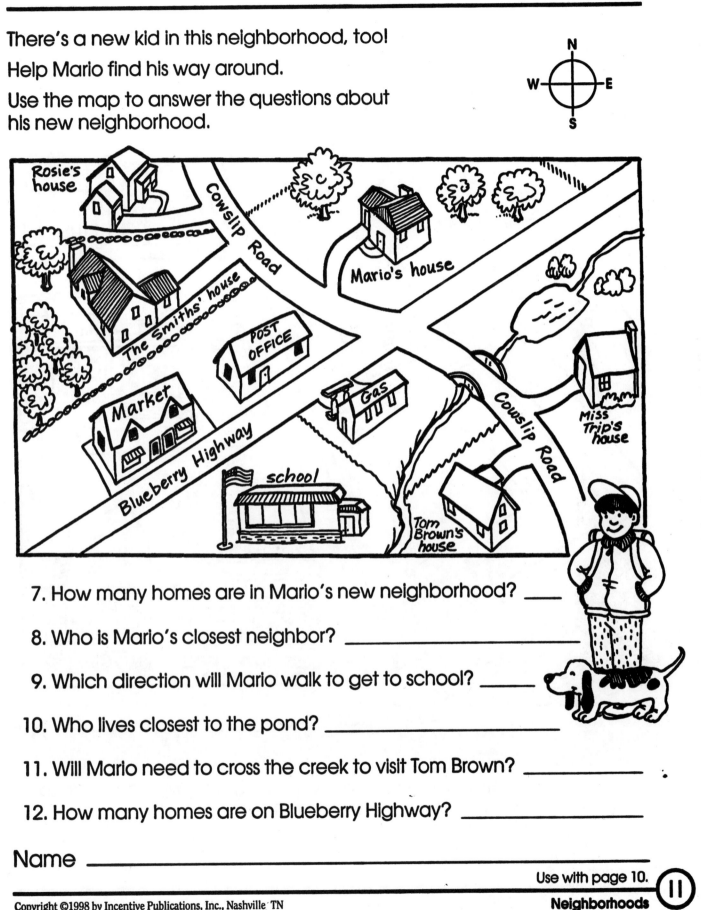

7. How many homes are in Mario's new neighborhood? ____

8. Who is Mario's closest neighbor? _____

9. Which direction will Mario walk to get to school? _____

10. Who lives closest to the pond? _____

11. Will Mario need to cross the creek to visit Tom Brown? _____

12. How many homes are on Blueberry Highway? _____

Name _____

Where Would You Go?

Where would you go to catch a fish, eat a pizza, or get a tooth fixed?

Towns and cities are full of places you can go to get things or do things.

Use the map of this town to decide where you would go to get or do the things listed on the next page (page 13).

Use with page 13.

Places in the Community

Basic Skills/Social Studies 2-3

Where Would You Go? cont.

Write the number of the place that you would go to . . .

1. borrow a book _____
2. get a car repaired _____
3. save some money _____
4. swing on a swing _____
5. see a ball game _____
6. buy a dog collar _____
7. eat a pizza _____
8. get your tooth fixed _____

9. rent a movie _____
10. attend a math class _____
11. practice your diving _____
12. practice your bowling _____
13. get a jacket cleaned _____
14. get rid of old newspapers _____
15. have knee surgery _____
16. drink a milkshake _____

Name _____

Use with page 12.

Places in the Community

Take a Hike . . . or Take a Bike!

There are many ways to get around a town.
You might choose your feet, a bike, a train, or a helicopter!
Look at the different kinds of transportation Abby finds in her town.
Which kind should she use for each place she wants to go?

Write the number to tell what Abby might use to . . .

1. get across the river _____

2. get across town _____

3. get out of town _____

4. get to the airport _____

5. take a baby for a stroll _____

6. look around the park _____

7. see the town
   from up in the air _____

8. visit Molly two
   blocks away _____

9. visit Grandma
   1000 miles away _____

10. get some
    good exercise _____

11. travel around town
    on sidewalks _____

12. enjoy an afternoon
    on the river _____

Name _____

Basic Skills/Social Studies 2-3

Don't Ignore the Signs!

They don't talk, but they tell you all kinds of important things!
Most of them are not even very big, but they give big messages!
We would be in big trouble without signs to let us know
what's what, what's where, what to do, and what not to do!
Every community has lots of signs.

Draw a line to match each of these with the word that
tells its meaning.

school crossing

poison

steep stairs

telephone

no smoking

wash your hands

slippery pavement

handicapped access

first aid

rest rooms

NO DOGS ALLOWED

Uh, oh!

Design a sign that
would give each
of these messages.

no littering

zoo

quiet

Name _____

Who's in Charge Here?

Valerie Tyler won the election! She is the new mayor of Grover City.
Roberto Sanchez is a new member of the city council.
What will they do in their new jobs?

City Council
Meeting Tonight

The **city council** is a group of people who have been elected by the citizens of the city to make rules and laws for the community. The council talks about problems and tries to solve them. They listen to citizens to hear what is important to them.

Agenda
- ✓ traffic problems
- ✓ plans for saving water
- ✓ build a new swimming pool?
- ✓ new skateboarding rules
- ✓ listening to citizens

The **mayor** helps to see that the laws are followed. He or she works with the council and many others to run the city.

1. Who is your mayor? _____

2. How long has he or she been the mayor? _____

3. How often does your community elect a mayor? _____

4. What group makes laws or rules in your community? _____

_____

5. Find the names of two people in that group. _____

and _____

Name _____

Show Me the Money

Where does the money go?

The citizens of Grover City want to know what happens to their tax money.
In most cities people pay taxes to help pay for services that everyone uses.
Here's how some of the money gets used in Grover City.

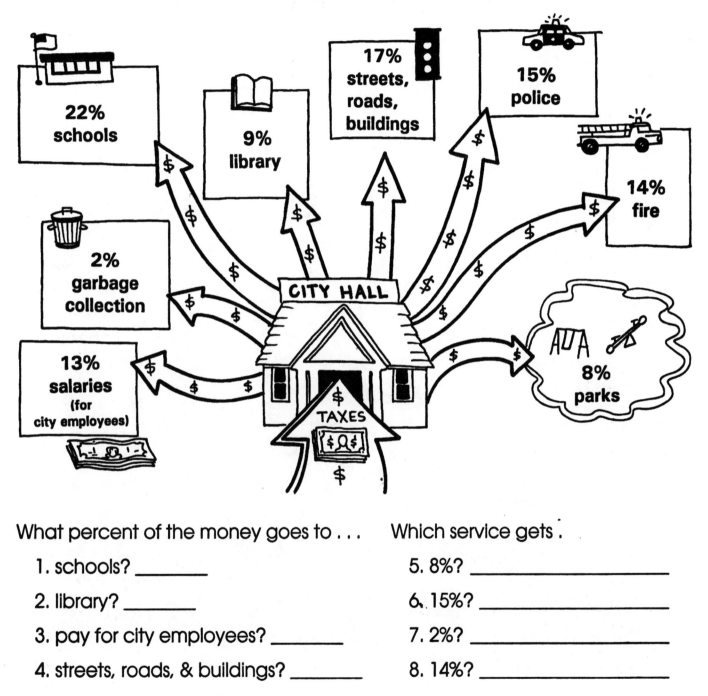

What percent of the money goes to . . .

1. schools? _____

2. library? _____

3. pay for city employees? _____

4. streets, roads, & buildings? _____

Which service gets :

5. 8%? _____

6. 15%? _____

7. 2%? _____

8. 14%? _____

Name _____

Taxes & Community Services

Who Can You Call?

Help!

There are many community services that can help you with different needs.
Which one should you call for each problem below?
Draw a line to match each need with the place that meets it.

1. You need help finding a fact for your history homework.

2. You see a fire out your window.

3. You find a lost child in the street.

4. You want to use the park picnic area for your soccer team party.

5. You see water gushing out of a pipe in the street.

6. Someone has been badly hurt.

7. You need to find a zip code.

8. Your garbage has not been picked up for three weeks.

9. There is a dangerous dog loose in your neighborhood.

10. The electricity has gone out on your street.

Post Office
Police
Garbage Collection
Library
Power Company
Ambulance
Woof! Woof!
Water Services
Animal Control
Fire Department
Parks Office

Name _____ _____

Is It a Law?

A **LAW** is a rule for a community. Everyone in the community must obey the laws. There are punishments for people who break laws.	A **RULE** is a statement about how people should behave.

It is not a good idea to throw food, but is there a law against it?

Figure it out! Learn the difference between a rule and a law.

Communities need both to help keep people safe and healthy and to help people live together, solve problems, and make decisions.

Look at each sign, and decide if it is a rule or law. Color the signs that show laws.

Name _____

We Do It This Way!

Families, communities, and other groups have customs.
A **custom** is a special way of doing things.

Every summer, Mario's family has a lightning bug party.

They invite all the neighbors to come for an after-dark picnic. They eat good food, play games, and catch lightning bugs. (Then they always set the lightning bugs free!)

Circle the customs that you have taken part in.

Thanksgiving dinner

Mardi Gras celebration

keeping a cricket in a cage

fireworks on July 4th

dressing up for a costume party

decorating Easter eggs

telling stories around a campfire

saluting the flag

breaking a piñata

lighting a menorah

reading a bedtime story

hanging stockings on a fireplace

decorating a Christmas tree

making valentines

making snow angels

Name _____

Basic Skills/Social Studies 2-3

Do You Really Need That?

Abby and Mario are packing for a camping trip.

They are going with their dads to spend two weeks living out in the woods.

What do they really need for survival?

Look at the things Abby and Mario are packing.

Color the things that are needs.

Needs are things humans must have in order to live (like food, clothing, shelter, air, water, and love).

Wants are things people would like to have but do not really need for survival.

Name _____

Workers Wanted!

The Grover City community bulletin board has ads for job openings.
Who can fill the jobs?
Write the number for each job next to the person who should apply for it.
Use the workers named in the box below.

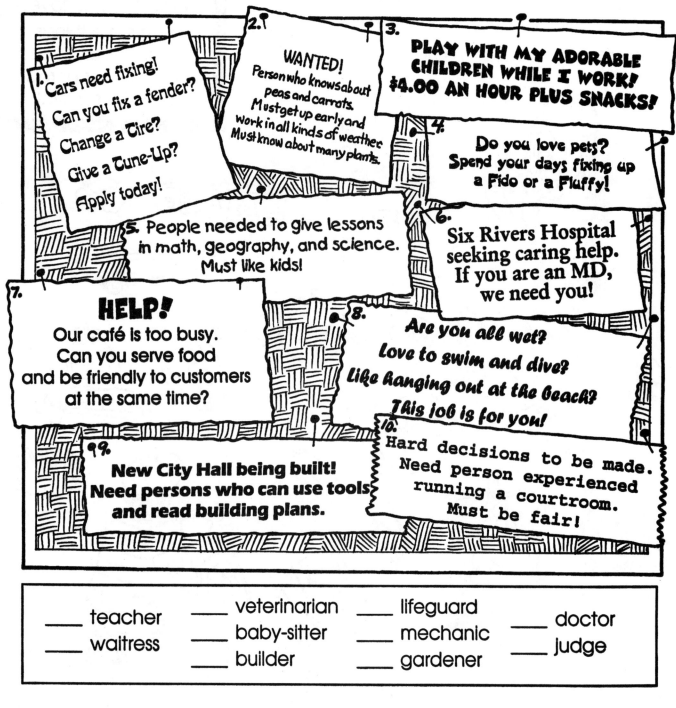

1. Cars need fixing! Can you fix a fender? Change a Tire? Give a Tune-Up? Apply today!

2. WANTED! Person who knows about peas and carrots. Must get up early and work in all kinds of weather. Must know about many plants.

3. PLAY WITH MY ADORABLE CHILDREN WHILE I WORK! $4.00 AN HOUR PLUS SNACKS!

4. Do you love pets? Spend your days fixing up a Fido or a Fluffy!

5. People needed to give lessons in math, geography, and science. Must like kids!

6. Six Rivers Hospital seeking caring help. If you are an MD, we need you!

7. HELP! Our café is too busy. Can you serve food and be friendly to customers at the same time?

8. Are you all wet? Love to swim and dive? Like hanging out at the beach? This job is for you!

9. New City Hall being built! Need persons who can use tools and read building plans.

10. Hard decisions to be made. Need person experienced running a courtroom. Must be fair!

___ teacher   ___ veterinarian   ___ lifeguard   ___ doctor
___ waitress   ___ baby-sitter   ___ mechanic   ___ judge
              ___ builder   ___ gardener

Name _____

Job Search

Copyright ©1998 by Incentive Publications, Inc., Nashville, TN.
Basic Skills/Social Studies 2-3

Jobs • Goods & Services

Name _____

Where Does Our Money Go?

So many things cost money! How does a family afford everything they need?

Abby's family is wondering why their money disappears so fast!

They made a graph to show how the money was used last month.

The family earned $1800 last month after they paid their taxes.

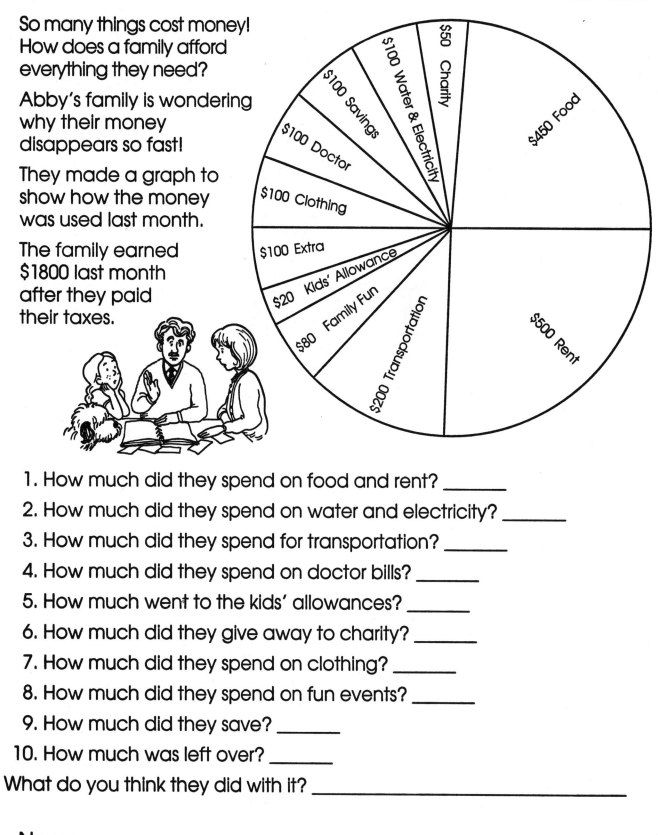

1. How much did they spend on food and rent? _____

2. How much did they spend on water and electricity? _____

3. How much did they spend for transportation? _____

4. How much did they spend on doctor bills? _____

5. How much went to the kids' allowances? _____

6. How much did they give away to charity? _____

7. How much did they spend on clothing? _____

8. How much did they spend on fun events? _____

9. How much did they save? _____

10. How much was left over? _____

What do you think they did with it? _____

Name _____

Where Did My Money Go?

Abby saved $30 from her allowance, birthday presents, and jobs.
She spent most of it. Now she is wondering where all her money went!
She's making a chart to see how she spent her money.
Color in the correct number of bars to show the amount she spent on each thing.

How I Spent My Money

		$1	$2	$3	$4	$5	$6	$7	$8	$9	$10
stickers	$2	▓	▓								
baseball cap	$8										
birthday present for Sasha	$3										
candy & ice cream	$1										
toy for dog	$4										
movie	$2										

1. What did she spend the most money on? _____

2. How much money does she have left over? _____

3. Below are some things she would like to buy. Can she get them all? _____

4. Circle one or more things she can afford to buy. The total cannot be more than $10.00.

cool poster	candy necklace	comic books	picture album
$4.00	$1.00	$2.00	$5.00

Name _____

Nature Gets Things Started

Things found in nature that people use are called **natural resources.** Many natural resources are used to make foods and other products.

Where does your orange juice really come from?

Where did your ice cream sundae begin?

Where did your peanut butter sandwich get started?

Many of the things we use, eat, wear, and enjoy come from nature.

Draw a line to connect each product (on the right) with the natural resource (on the left) that was used to produce it.

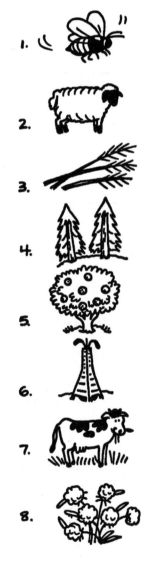

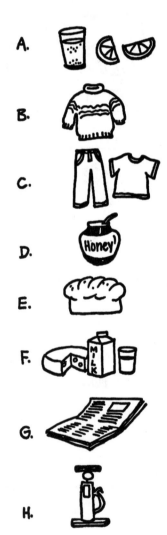

Name _____

Resources & Products

Getting Ice Cream from a Cow

How do you get ice cream from a cow? It takes some work!

Most of the foods and products we buy must be grown or manufactured.

Draw a path from each resource to the place where the product is made and then to the product.

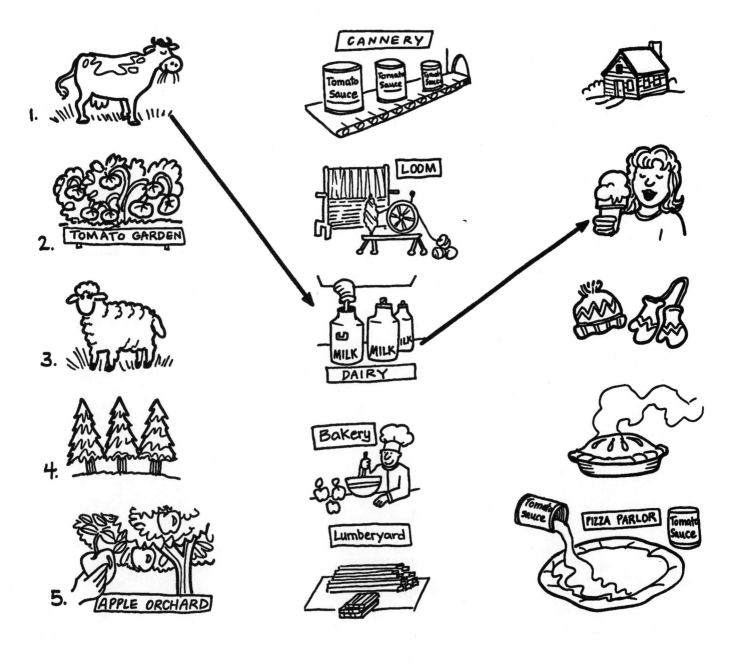

Name _____

The Case of the Missing States

Something is missing from Mario's map! All the states that begin with **A, F, O,** and **T** are missing their names. Can you put them back?

1. Find your own state. Color it red.

2. The names of these cities are missing. Write their names where they belong:

        Chicago   New York   San Francisco   Miami

3. Find a state that touches the Atlantic Ocean. Color it green.

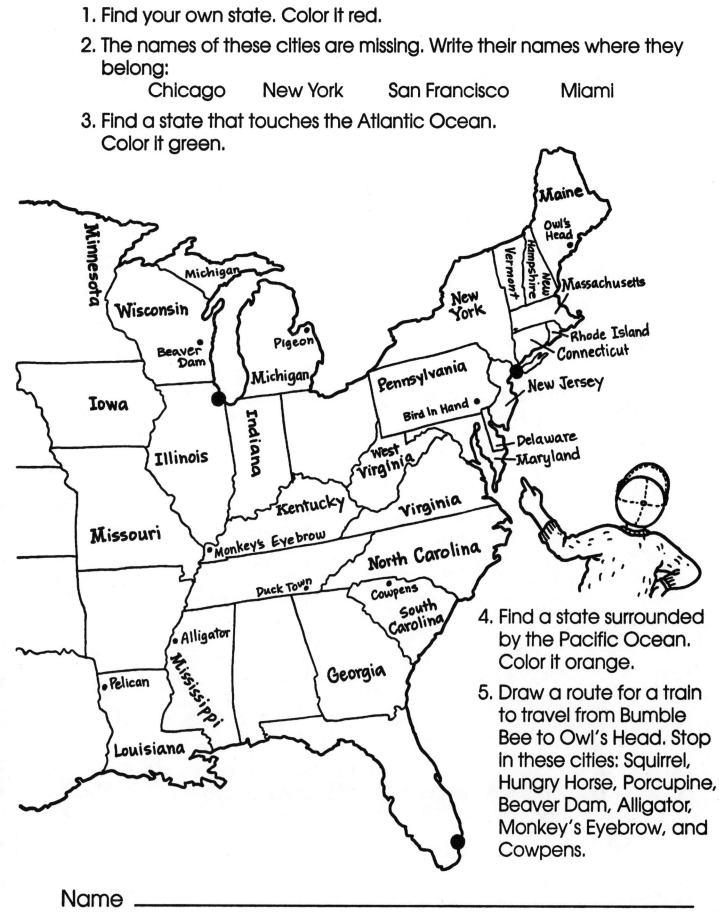

4. Find a state surrounded by the Pacific Ocean. Color it orange.

5. Draw a route for a train to travel from Bumble Bee to Owl's Head. Stop in these cities: Squirrel, Hungry Horse, Porcupine, Beaver Dam, Alligator, Monkey's Eyebrow, and Cowpens.

Name _____

U.S. Map • Recognize States

Far-out State Facts

Which state had the first pizza parlor?
Which state has "Yankee Doodle" as its state song?
Which state has the largest volcano?

You can find out right now—if you know the shapes of the states in the USA!

Look at the shape of each state below and find it on the map (page 31).

Color the state on the map, and then write its name on the line.

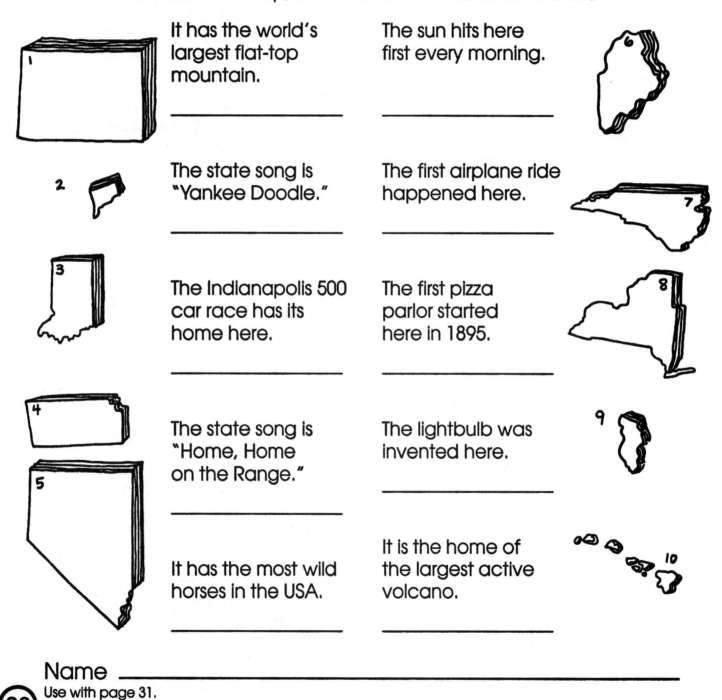

It has the world's largest flat-top mountain.

_____

The state song is "Yankee Doodle."

_____

The Indianapolis 500 car race has its home here.

_____

The state song is "Home, Home on the Range."

_____

It has the most wild horses in the USA.

_____

The sun hits here first every morning.

_____

The first airplane ride happened here.

_____

The first pizza parlor started here in 1895.

_____

The lightbulb was invented here.

_____

It is the home of the largest active volcano.

_____

Name _____

The United States

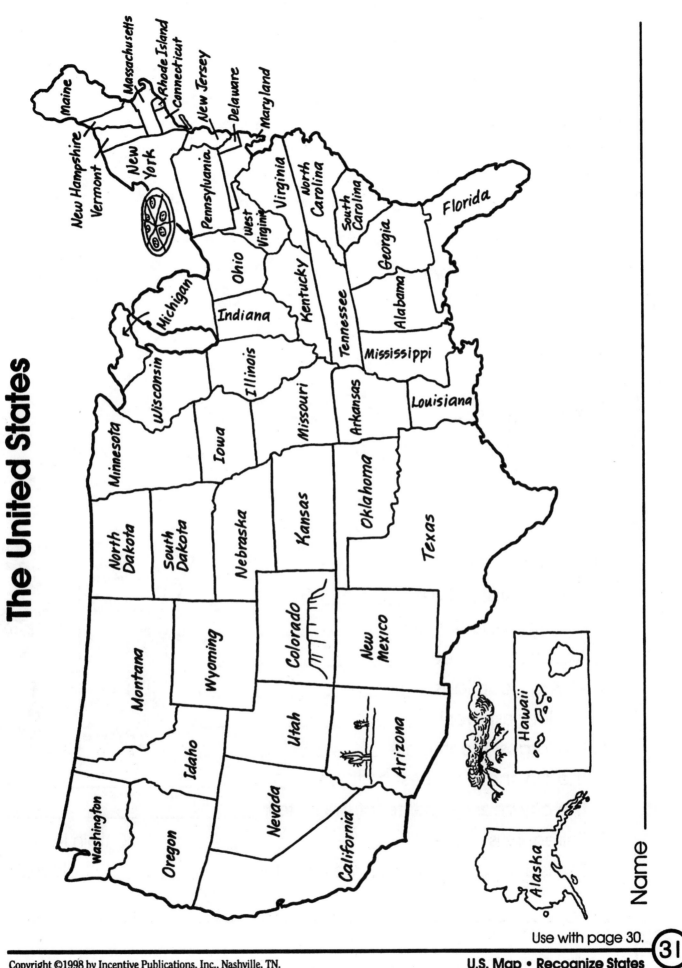

Maine
New Hampshire
Vermont
Massachusetts
Rhode Island
Connecticut
New Jersey
Delaware
Maryland
New York
Pennsylvania
West Virginia
Virginia
North Carolina
South Carolina
Florida
Ohio
Kentucky
Tennessee
Georgia
Alabama
Mississippi
Louisiana
Michigan
Indiana
Illinois
Wisconsin
Missouri
Arkansas
Minnesota
Iowa
Oklahoma
Texas
North Dakota
South Dakota
Nebraska
Kansas
Montana
Wyoming
Colorado
New Mexico
Idaho
Utah
Arizona
Washington
Oregon
Nevada
California
Hawaii
Alaska

U.S. Map • **Recognize States**

Name

Amazing Alaska

Did you know that Alaska is the biggest and the coldest state?
Did you know that it contains the highest mountain in the United States?
Alaska is an amazing place full of forests, grizzly bears, beautiful lakes, mountains, and glaciers.
Use the map to find out more about amazing Alaska!

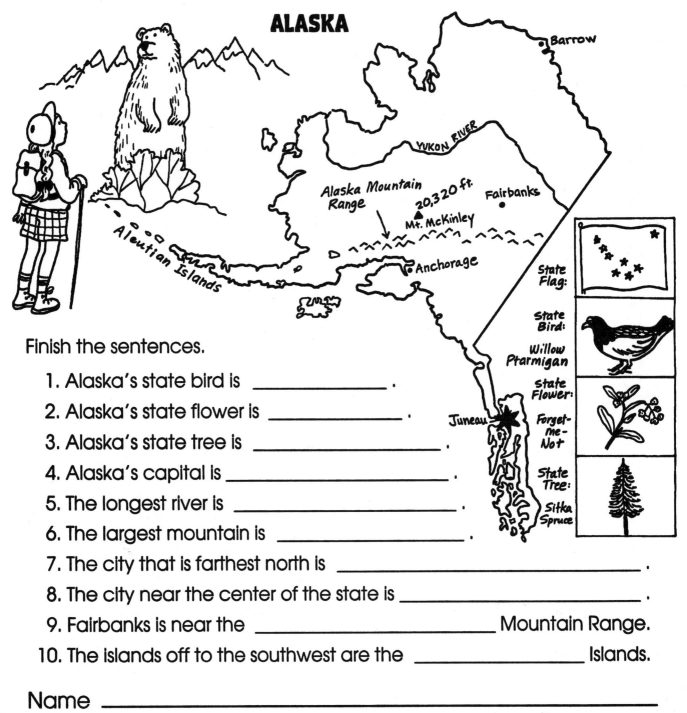

Finish the sentences.

1. Alaska's state bird is _____ .

2. Alaska's state flower is _____ .

3. Alaska's state tree is _____ .

4. Alaska's capital is _____ .

5. The longest river is _____ .

6. The largest mountain is _____ .

7. The city that is farthest north is _____ .

8. The city near the center of the state is _____ .

9. Fairbanks is near the _____ Mountain Range.

10. The islands off to the southwest are the _____ Islands.

Name _____

Copyright ©1998 by Incentive Publications, Inc., Nashville, TN.
Basic Skills/Social Studies 2-3

Your Amazing State

What is amazing about your state?

Does it have the highest bridge in the world, the first library, the only diamond mine in the USA, or the most people?

Every state in the USA has some amazing places, spaces, and facts to know about it. See what you can find out about your own state!

My state has the deepest lake in the U.S.A.!

1. Draw your state here.

2. Put your town or city on the map.

3. Put the capital city on the map.

4. Add other cities, a river, a mountain, or some other features of your state.

5. Find and draw the state symbols on the right.

6. Find out one amazing thing about your state. _____

State Flag:	State Bird:
State Flower:	State Tree:

Name _____

Make a State Map

Where's the Party?

Roberto is headed to a party!

On his way, he is picking up food and other great stuff.

He is getting these things from the United States and its neighbors.

Read about each stop he makes, and look at the map on page 35.

Draw his route in red on the map as he travels to collect these things . . .

1. hats from his country, Panama

2. coconuts from Costa Rica

3. sugar cubes from Nicaragua

4. bananas from El Salvador and Honduras

5. flowers from the island country of Jamaica

6. tasty lobsters from Belize

7. bright-colored tablecloths from Guatemala

8. candy-filled piñatas from Mexico

9. pizza from San Francisco, California

10. fresh salmon from Alaska

11. hamburgers from Winnipeg, Canada

12. ice cubes from Greenland

13. French pastries from Quebec, Canada

14. clams from Boston, Massachusetts

15. key lime pie from Miami, Florida

16. musical instruments from Haiti

17. sugar cookies from Cuba

18. chocolates from the Bahamas

19. a camera from the Dominican Republic

20. At last! Roberto has arrived with all his stuff!

    The party is on the island that is farthest east.

    Where is the party? _____

Name _____

The United States & Its Neighbors

Name _____

A Map of Ups & Downs

Mario's class has made a map that shows the ups and downs on the Earth's surface. They put little flags on the map to show different landforms.

Do you know which landform is which?

Write the number from the correct flag next to the word for each landform.

bay ☐   island ☐   plain ☐

river ☐   lake ☐   beach ☐   valley ☐

peninsula ☐   mountain ☐   plateau ☐   ocean ☐

Name _____

Copyright ©1998 by Incentive Publications, Inc., Nashville, TN.
Basic Skills/Social Studies 2-3

Spin the Globe

Abby and Mario are spinning their globes to see where they stop.

When they stop, the kids are looking for the continents that are in different hemispheres. (A hemisphere is half of the Earth!)

Help them find the continents in each hemisphere. Look at both globes.

Eastern Hemisphere

Western Hemisphere

Eastern Hemisphere

Southern Hemisphere

Western Hemisphere

Northern Hemisphere

Name _____

Where Would You Find It?

Detective Bones travels the world to track down amazing things and places.

These are things he is searching for now.

Circle the place where he will probably find each of them.

1. Grand Canyon
   a. under the Atlantic Ocean
   b. in Africa
   c. in Arizona

2. great floating icebergs
   a. in the Arctic Ocean
   b. in every ocean
   c. in Lake Michigan

3. Eiffel Tower
   a. in Texas
   b. in Paris, France
   c. in Tokyo, Japan

4. Panama Canal
   a. in Africa
   b. across Australia
   c. in Central America

5. Mississippi River
   a. in Canada
   b. in the United States
   c. in South America

6. world's tallest mountain
   a. in Alaska
   b. in Turkey
   c. in Antarctica

7. islands of Japan
   a. in the Atlantic Ocean
   b. in the Arctic Ocean
   c. in the Pacific Ocean

8. Statue of Liberty
   a. in Boston
   b. in London
   c. in New York City

9. Sahara Desert
   a. in north Africa
   b. in South America
   c. in Russia

10. Great Wall
    a. in California
    b. in China
    c. in Spain

11. Indian Ocean
    a. near North America
    b. near South America
    c. near Africa

12. great pyramids
    a. in Florida
    b. in Egypt
    c. in France

Name _____

Copyright ©1998 by Incentive Publications, Inc., Nashville, TN.
Basic Skills/Social Studies 2-3

Mix-up in the Mail Room

Miss Martha works for the post office.
It is her job to sort the mail.

Help her sort the letters.

Find the mail that is addressed to cities and color it green.
Find the mail that is addressed to states and color it blue.
Find the mail that is addressed to countries and color it red.
Find the mail that is addressed to continents
and color it yellow.

Name _____

Cities, States, Countries, & Continents

Worldwide Pen Pals

Abby writes to eight pen pals all over the world each month.

Read about her pen pals.

Draw a line from each pen pal to the place on the map where he or she lives.

Then label the continents of the world.

James is from Canada. This country is just north of the United States.

James

Juanita's country is Mexico. It is the neighbor to the south of the United States.

Juanita

Bonita lives in Bolivia. Bolivia is on the continent of South America.

Bonita

Name _____

Use with page 41.

Ivan is Russian. His country is a large one! It is in both Europe and Asia!

Tomoyuki's country is Japan. It is made up of islands.

Ivan

Fiona

Fiona is from Ireland. It is an island country of Europe.

Saja

Tomoyuki

Saja lives in a hot country in Africa. Her country is Algeria.

Gigi

Australia is where Gigi lives. Her country is also a continent!

Name _____

Follow the Flags

The athletes are getting ready for the Olympic Games!
They come from many countries all over the world.
Each athlete is carrying the flag from his or her country.
Read each description, and then write the letter of the matching flag beside it.

_____ 1. China's flag has one big star and four small stars.

_____ 2. Turkey's flag has a moon and a star.

_____ 3. Canada has a maple leaf on its flag.

_____ 4. Chile's flag has one star.

_____ 5. Great Britain's flag has four stripes that cross each other.

_____ 6. Congo's flag has a diagonal yellow stripe across the middle.

Name _____

World Cultures • Read a Diagram

_____ 7. Peru's flag has two wide red stripes and one white stripe.

_____ 8. South Africa's flag has a big green Y lying on its side!

_____ 9. Korea's flag has a large red and blue circle in the center.

_____ 10. The flag of Finland has a blue cross on a white background.

_____ 11. Panama's flag has two stars.

_____ 12. The flag of the USA has 50 stars and 13 stripes.

Color each flag on pages 42 and 43 with the right colors!

Name _____

Use with page 42.

The Government Tree

The third graders have discovered that the United States government is like a tree because it has branches.

They have drawn a tree to show the three branches of government.

Study the tree. Then answer the questions below.

The Three Branches of Government

EXECUTIVE BRANCH
PRESIDENT & VICE PRESIDENT
See that the laws are followed
Elected every 4 years

LEGISLATIVE BRANCH
CONGRESS
Makes the laws

House of Representatives
1 or more from each state
Elected for 2 years
Senate
2 from each state
Elected for 6 years

JUDICIAL BRANCH
SUPREME COURT
Sees that the laws are fair
9 members, lifelong term
Appointed by the president

1. Who is the president? _____

2. Who is the vice president? _____

3. Name one senator or
   representative from your state. _____

4. Name one member of
   the U.S. Supreme Court. _____

Name _____

Eagles, Bells, & Fireworks

Eagles, bells, and fireworks are all part of American tradition.

The eagle is a national symbol. The Liberty Bell is a symbol of freedom.

Fireworks are used to celebrate the day the United States became a nation!

All the squares on the grid show symbols, holidays, places, or things that are important parts of American tradition.

Write the location for each item, showing the square's letter and number.

Color all the blank squares red or blue.

Write the location for each one.

1. Liberty Bell _A, 3_

2. Pilgrim _____

3. Declaration of Independence _____

4. Eagle _____

5. Abe Lincoln _____

6. USA Flag _____

7. Uncle Sam _____

8. Capitol Building _____

9. Washington Monument _____

10. Fireworks _____

11. Statue of Liberty _____

12. George Washington _____

Name _____

Your Fantasy Country

Have you ever wanted to invent your own country?

Well, here's your chance to think about what kind of country you would create.

Who would be the leader?
What laws would there be?

What rights would people have?
How would tax money be used?

Follow the directions to design your fantasy country.

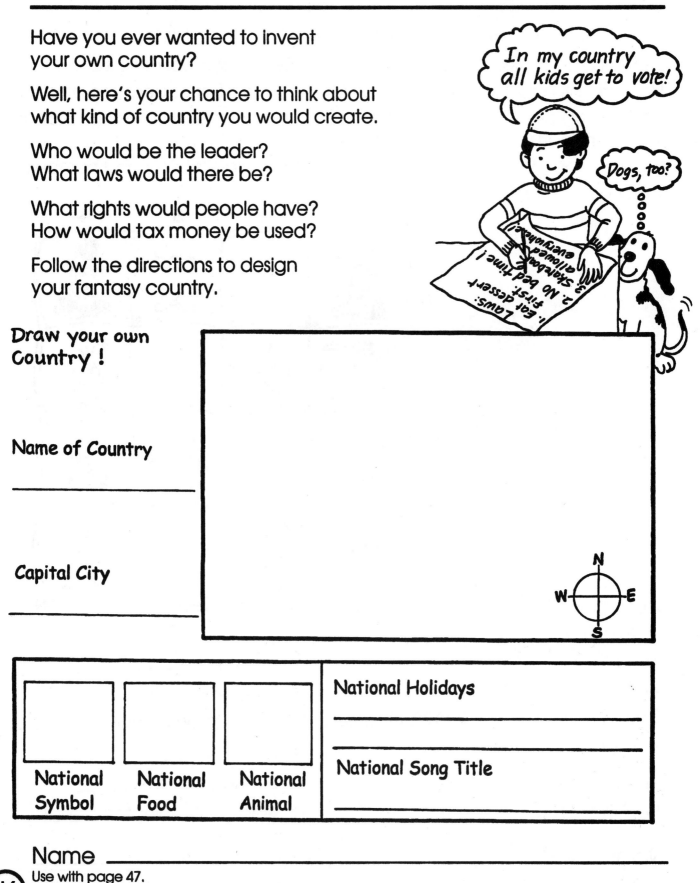

In my country all kids get to vote!

Dogs, too?

Laws:
1. Eat dessert first.
2. No bed time!
3. Skateboards allowed everywhere!

Draw your own Country !

Name of Country

_____

Capital City

_____

N
W   E
S

National Symbol

National Food

National Animal

National Holidays

_____

_____

National Song Title

_____

Name _____

Citizens' Rights

$ TAXES $

Tax money will be used for.....

LAWS

LEADERS

Draw your own flag.

Old Flag, New Flag

The United States flag we use today is not the same as the first flag!
These kids are painting large pictures of the first flag and the latest flag.
Help them by filling in the color in the right places on both flags.
Look at a picture of these flags to help you find the right colors.
How many stars and stripes are on each flag?

The first U.S. flag was made in 1777.

This flag had:

_____ red stripes

_____ white stripes

_____ stars

The flag has changed 26 times.
This is the flag used since 1959.
This flag has:

_____ red stripes

_____ white stripes

_____ stars

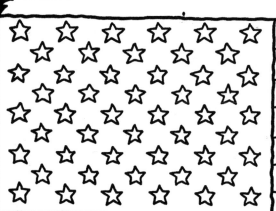

Name _____

Basic Skills/Social Studies 2-3

Which Happened First?

Look at the giant timeline of U.S. history!
Use the timeline to find out when things happened.

1. Which happened first?
   a. Telephone invented
   b. First airplane ride
   c. Abe Lincoln elected

2. Which happened first?
   a. Women vote
   b. Gold discovered
   c. Kennedy elected

3. Which happened first?
   a. U.S. is born
   b. Pilgrims arrive
   c. Washington elected

4. Which happened first?
   a. Statue of Liberty arrives
   b. Telephone invented
   c. First moon walk

5. Which happened first?
   a. U.S. 200th birthday
   b. First moon walk
   c. Women vote

6. Which happened **last?**
   a. First moon walk
   b. Statue of Liberty arrives
   c. U.S. 200th Birthday

7. Which happened **last?**
   a. Kennedy elected
   b. Lincoln elected
   c. Washington elected

1620	PILGRIMS ARRIVE
1776	THE U.S. IS BORN
1789	GEORGE WASHINGTON BECOMES FIRST PRESIDENT
1848	GOLD DISCOVERED IN CALIFORNIA
1860	ABE LINCOLN BECOMES 16TH U.S. PRESIDENT
1876	TELEPHONE INVENTED
1886	FRANCE GIVES U.S. THE STATUE OF LIBERTY
1903	FIRST AIRPLANE RIDE
1920	WOMEN GET THE RIGHT TO VOTE
1960	KENNEDY ELECTED PRESIDENT
1969	FIRST MOON WALK
1976	200TH BIRTHDAY FOR U.S.

Name _____

U.S. History • Timeline

Headlines from the Past

Newspaper headlines announce major events in any country. These headlines give news of some events in American history. Read the headlines to help you complete the sentences below.

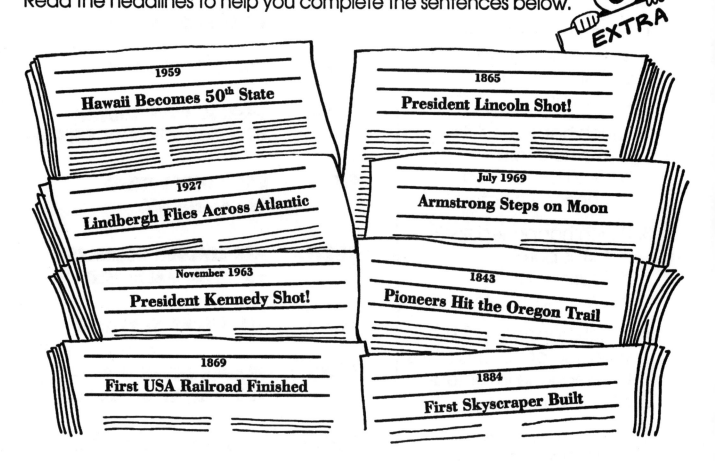

1959
Hawaii Becomes 50ᵗʰ State

1865
President Lincoln Shot!

1927
Lindbergh Flies Across Atlantic

July 1969
Armstrong Steps on Moon

November 1963
President Kennedy Shot!

1843
Pioneers Hit the Oregon Trail

1869
First USA Railroad Finished

1884
First Skyscraper Built

1. President Kennedy was shot about _____ years after President Lincoln.

2. Circle the one that was built first: the first U.S. railroad   the first skyscraper

3. Did Hawaii become a state before the first moon walk? yes no

4. What year did Charles Lindbergh cross the Atlantic Ocean? _____

5. Was the first skyscraper built before Kennedy was president? yes no

6. Was the Oregon Trail made before the first cross-country railroad? yes no

7. What year was the first cross-country railroad finished? _____

8. Who took the first step on the moon? _____

Name _____

Headlines from the Present

Newspaper headlines still announce important events!
Write headlines to tell about things happening
in your school, your town, your state, or your country.
Write the date on the first line of each paper.
Write a short headline on the second line.

Name _____

Some Very Important Americans

It's library day! Abby needs to choose a biography to read.
She is looking for a biography of a famous American, but she is not sure what to choose! Help her find out about these books.
Write the number of each book next to its description.

____ A. the first U.S. president

____ B. explorers who established a route to the West Coast

____ C. nurse who began the American Red Cross

____ D. Indian woman who led explorers to the West Coast

____ E. the 16th U.S. president, who was born in a log cabin

____ F. black leader who gave the famous "I have a dream" speech

____ G. American scientist who did experiments with electricity

____ H. Nez Perce Indian chief who tried to help his tribe escape to Canada

____ I. first woman in the U.S. to become an astronaut

____ J. black woman who would not give up her bus seat to a white person

Name _____

Copyright ©1998 by INCENTIVE PUBLICATIONS, Inc., Nashville, TN.
Basic Skills/Social Studies 2-3

Citizens on Parade

The kids are showing off their signs about good citizens.
They forgot to finish some of the signs!
Finish the signs for them.
Make each sign tell
something about
a good citizen.

A good citizen
helps others.

Show you
care about
your city.
Keep it
clean!

A good citizen does
not waste the Earth's
valuable resources.

Good citizens
remember
to vote!

Name _____

Getting around Washington, DC

Do you know how to get to the White House?

Could you find the Washington Monument?

Find your way around the nation's capital with the help of this map!

Use the map on page 55 to locate some of the things in the United States capital city of Washington, DC.

1. What street goes to the White House? _____

2. What street goes from the
White House to the Capitol? _____

3. Circle the monuments that are close to the Potomac River.
   a. Lincoln Memorial
   b. Washington Monument
   c. Jefferson Memorial

4. Circle the two buildings that are east of the Capitol.
   a. Library of Congress
   b. Supreme Court
   c. Lincoln Memorial

5. Circle the buildings that are in the Mall
   a. The Supreme Court
   b. The Smithsonian Institution
   c. The Museum of Natural History

6. What street borders the Mall on the north?

   _____

7. What street borders the Mall on the south?

   _____

8. Name two places in Washington, DC, that you would like to visit.

   _____

   _____

Name _____

Map of Washington, DC

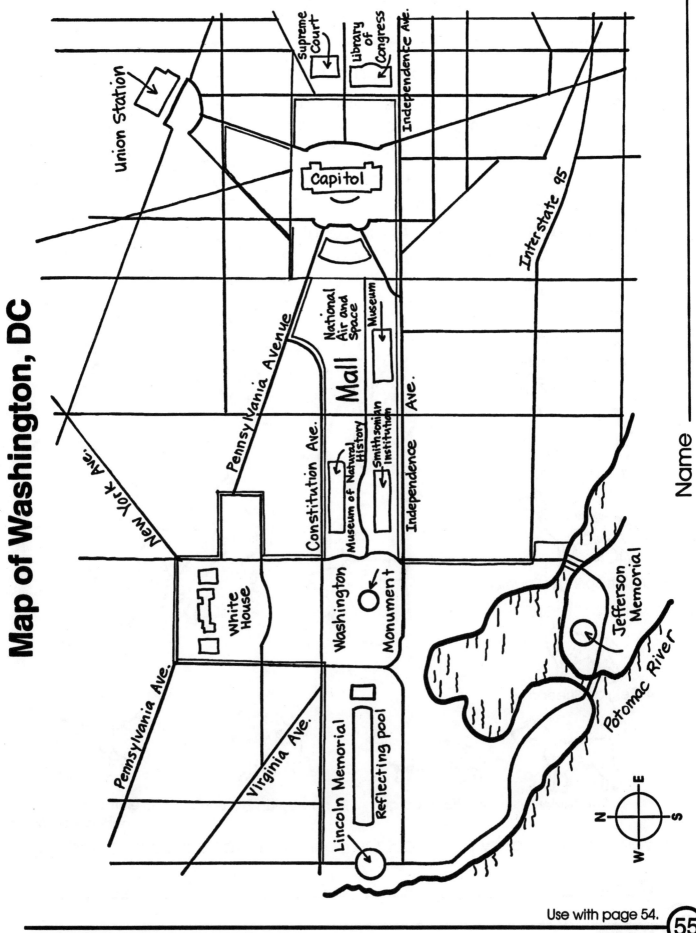

Union Station

Supreme Court

Library of Congress

Independence Ave.

Capitol

Interstate 95

Pennsylvania Avenue

National Air and Space Museum

Mall

Constitution Ave.

New York Ave.

Museum of Natural History

Smithsonian Institution

Independence Ave.

White House

Washington Monument

Pennsylvania Ave.

Virginia Ave.

Lincoln Memorial

Reflecting pool

Jefferson Memorial

Potomac River

Name

N E W S

It's a Dog's World!

Abby is wondering where her dog came from!

When she looks in a dog book, she learns that different breeds of dogs come from many countries all over the world!

One map in her book shows some of the dogs that came from Europe.

Draw a line from each dog to the country it matches, and then color the country.

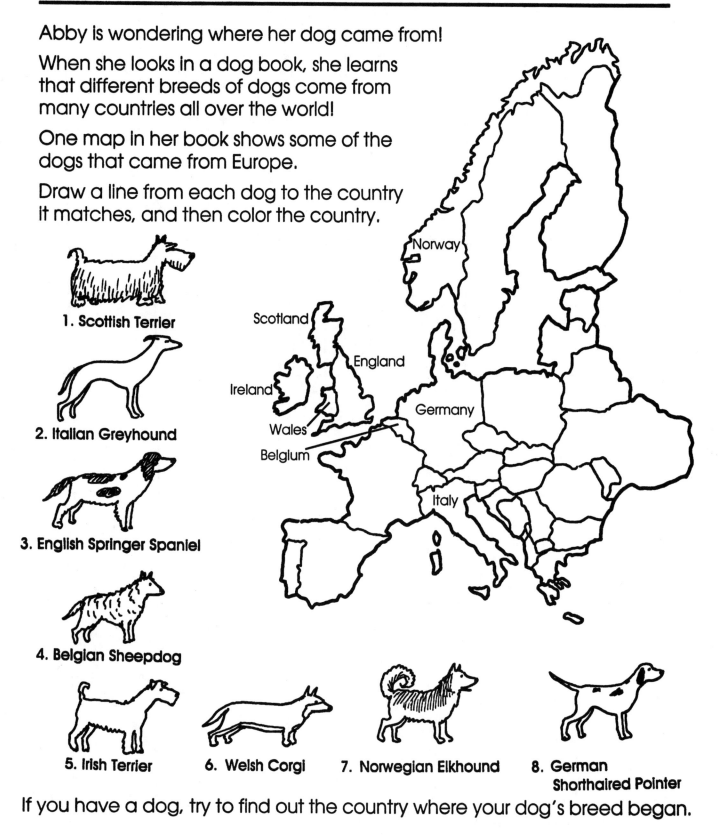

1. Scottish Terrier

2. Italian Greyhound

3. English Springer Spaniel

4. Belgian Sheepdog

5. Irish Terrier

6. Welsh Corgi

7. Norwegian Elkhound

8. German Shorthaired Pointer

Norway

Scotland

England

Ireland

Wales

Belgium

Germany

Italy

If you have a dog, try to find out the country where your dog's breed began.

Name _____

Millions Live in the Top 6

Wow! The top 6 biggest cities in the United States have a lot of people!
If you put them all together, these cities have over 18 million people.
Read the chart to answer the questions about the top 6.

POPULATION in the TOP 6 U.S. Cities	
New York	🚶🚶🚶🚶🚶🚶🚶
Los Angeles	🚶🚶🚶🚶
Chicago	🚶🚶🚶
Houston	🚶🚶
Philadelphia	🚶🚶
San Diego	🚶

🚶 = 1 million people

1. Which city has about 3 million people? _____

2. Which city has more people than Los Angeles? _____

3. About how many people live in Philadelphia? _____

4. About how many people live in Los Angeles? _____

5. Which city has about 1 million people? _____

6. Which city has about 2 million people? _____

7. About how many people live in New York City? _____

Find out the population of your town or city. _____

Name _____

Population Chart

Social Studies Skills Test

Circle the correct answer.

1. A place where people live and play and work is a
    neighborhood   government   history

2. A behavior that must be followed by everyone in a community is a
    rule   law   need   want

3. A place to go in a community to get a car fixed is a
    cleaners   bank   service station   hospital

4. A place to call to report a stolen bike is a
    recycling center   park   school   police station

5. A way to move from one place to another is called
    community   transportation   government

Choose the words that tell the meaning of each sign. Write the letter.

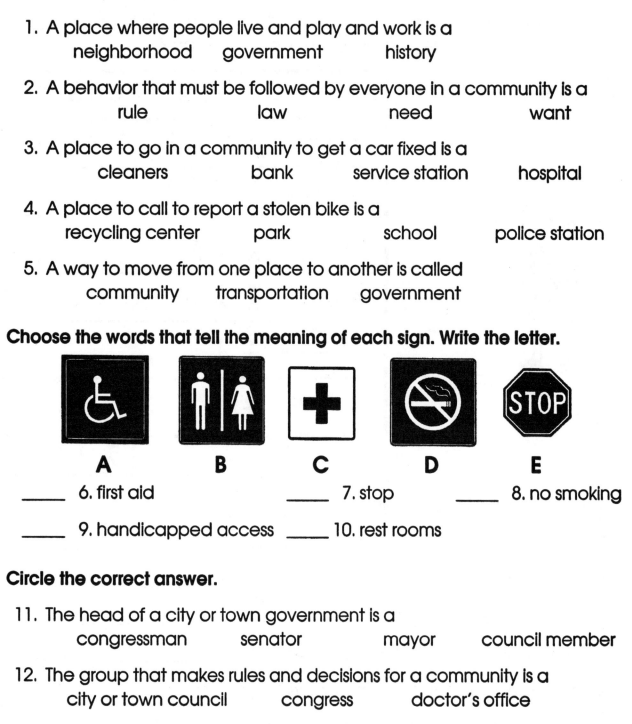

A   B   C   D   E

_____ 6. first aid   _____ 7. stop   _____ 8. no smoking

_____ 9. handicapped access   _____ 10. rest rooms

Circle the correct answer.

11. The head of a city or town government is a
    congressman   senator   mayor   council member

12. The group that makes rules and decisions for a community is a
    city or town council   congress   doctor's office

13. Something that city taxes would probably not be used for is
    schools   streets & roads   groceries   city parks

Name _____

Copyright ©1998 by Incentive Publications, Inc., Nashville, TN.
Basic Skills/Social Studies 2-3

14. Circle the sign that shows a law.

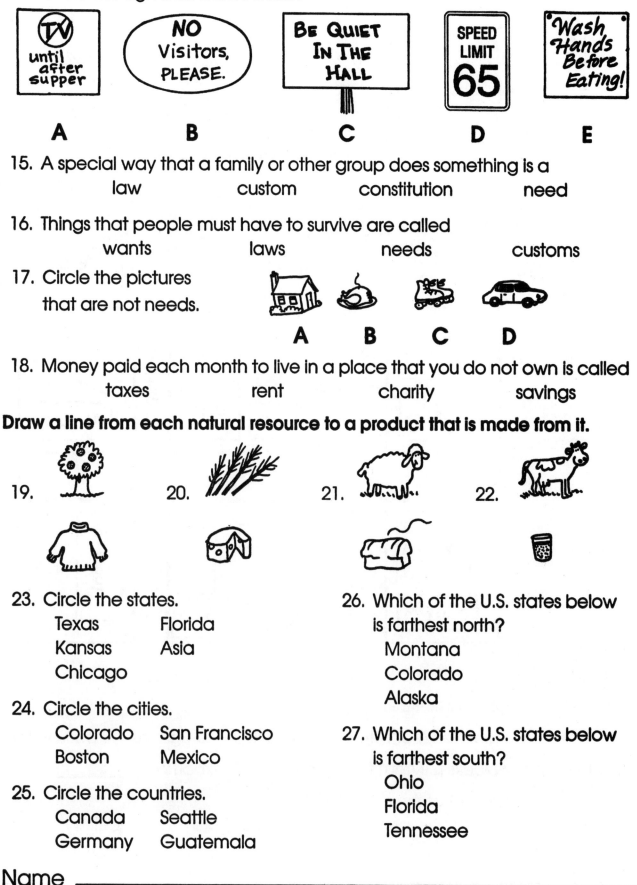

A   B   C   D   E

15. A special way that a family or other group does something is a

      law   custom   constitution   need

16. Things that people must have to survive are called

      wants   laws   needs   customs

17. Circle the pictures that are not needs.

A   B   C   D

18. Money paid each month to live in a place that you do not own is called

      taxes   rent   charity   savings

Draw a line from each natural resource to a product that is made from it.

19.   20.   21.   22.

23. Circle the states.
     Texas   Florida
     Kansas   Asia
     Chicago

24. Circle the cities.
     Colorado   San Francisco
     Boston   Mexico

25. Circle the countries.
     Canada   Seattle
     Germany   Guatemala

26. Which of the U.S. states below is farthest north?
     Montana
     Colorado
     Alaska

27. Which of the U.S. states below is farthest south?
     Ohio
     Florida
     Tennessee

Name _____

28. Circle the workers that are working to make or grow something.

A   B   C   D

29. Circle the workers that are doing a service for someone.

A   B   C   D

Use the map to answer the questions.

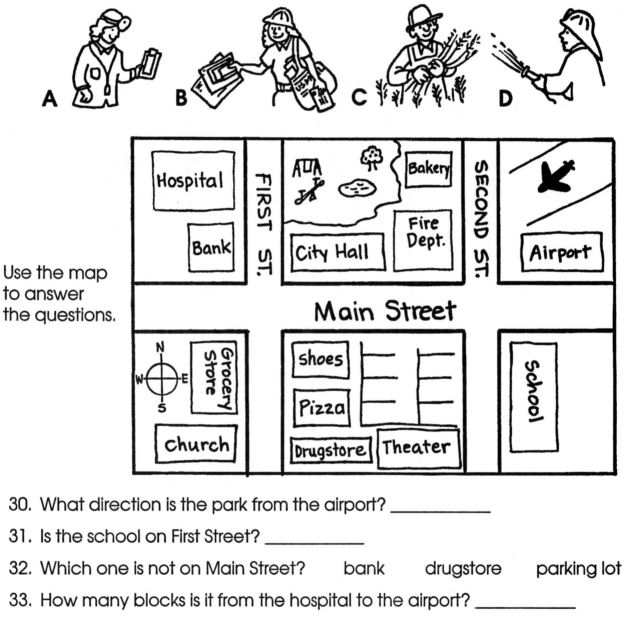

30. What direction is the park from the airport? _____

31. Is the school on First Street? _____

32. Which one is not on Main Street?   bank   drugstore   parking lot

33. How many blocks is it from the hospital to the airport? _____

34. What store is west of the shoe store?
grocery store   pizza shop   drugstore   bakery

Name _____

Circle the correct answer.

35. Which country is not a neighbor of the United States?
    Mexico   Canada   India   Costa Rica   Haiti

36. Which country is in South America?
    Canada   Russia   Bolivia   Germany

37. Which country is in Europe?
    France   Panama   China   Australia

38. Which country is in North America?
    Japan   United States   Ireland

39. Which part of the U.S. government makes the laws?
    the president   the Supreme Court   the Congress

40. Which happened first?
    the first airplane was flown   the first person stepped on the moon

41. Which happened last?
    Washington   Kennedy   Lincoln
    was president   was president   was president

42. Which building is not in Washington, DC?
    the Statue of Liberty   the Capitol Building   the Lincoln Memorial

Look at the grid. Write the location of each American symbol or monument.

_____ 43. flag

_____ 44. Statue of Liberty

_____ 45. eagle

_____ 46. White House

_____ 47. pilgrim

_____ 48. fireworks

_____ 49. Liberty Bell

_____ 50. Washington Monument

Name _____

Answer Key

Skills Test

1. neighborhood
2. law
3. service station
4. police station
5. transportation
6. C
7. E
8. D
9. A
10. B
11. mayor
12. city or town council
13. groceries
14. D
15. custom
16. needs
17. C and D
18. rent
19. orange juice
20. bread
21. sweater
22. cheese
23. Texas, Kansas, Florida
24. San Francisco, Boston
25. Canada, Germany, Guatemala
26. Alaska
27. Florida
28. B and C
29. A, B, and D
30. west
31. no
32. drugstore
33. 2
34. grocery store
35. India
36. Bolivia
37. France
38. United States
39. the Congress
40. the first airplane was flown
41. Kennedy was president
42. the Statue of Liberty
43. A, 3
44. A, 1
45. B, 3
46. B, 1
47. C, 3
48. C, 1
49. A, 2
50. C, 2

Skills Exercises

pages 10–11

1. 3
2. 3
3. 2
4. northeast
5. Jefferson
6. Jefferson and Tenth
7. 5
8. The Smiths
9. south
10. Miss Trip
11. yes
12. none

pages 12–13

1. 9	5. 8	9. 15	13. 2
2. 4	6. 17	10. 11	14. 14
3. 3	7. 19	11. 23	15. 21
4. 22	8. 24	12. 5	16. 10

page 14

Answers will vary. Students may give one or more answers for each. Possible answers are:

1. 1, 2, 3, 4, 7, 10, 13
2. 1, 2, 3, 4, 5, 7, 8, 9, 12
3. 1, 2, 3, 4, 5, 6, 10, 13
4. 2, 4, 5, 6, 7
5. 11, 12
6. 8, 9, 11, 12
7. 5, 6
8. 2, 4, 8, 9, 11, 12
9. 2, 4, 6
10. 8, 9, 12
11. 8, 9, 11, 12
12. 10, 13

page 15

Check to see that lines have been drawn to appropriate signs.
Students' own sign designs at bottom will vary.

page 16

Answers will vary.

page 17

1. 22%
2. 9%
3. 13%
4. 17%
5. parks
6. police
7. garbage collection
8. fire

page 18

1. library
2. fire department
3. police
4. parks office
5. water services
6. ambulance
7. post office
8. garbage collection
9. animal control
10. power company

page 19

Laws are:

Wrong Way	One Way
Do Not Enter	Stop
Private Property	Slow
Yield	Speed Limit 55

Copyright ©1998 by Incentive Publications, Inc., Nashville, TN.
Basic Skills/Social Studies 2-3

page 20
Answers will vary.

page 21
Answers may vary somewhat.
Needs:
crackers, cans of soup, raisins, apples, tent, canteens (water), hat, gloves, socks, clothing

page 22
1. mechanic
2. gardener
3. baby-sitter
4. veterinarian
5. teacher
6. doctor
7. waitress
8. lifeguard
9. builder
10. judge

page 23
Answers may vary, depending on interpretation of the jobs!
Goods path—red—farmer, auto maker, baker, artist, shoemaker, cook, tent maker, builder, gardener
Services path—green—librarian, doctor, janitor, piano teacher, animal trainer, auto salesman, grocery store clerk, mayor, president, waiter, plumber, banker, police woman, fireman, baseball player

page 24
1. $950
2. $100
3. $200
4. $100
5. $20
6. $50
7. $100
8. $80
9. $100
10. $100; Answers will vary.

page 25
1. baseball cap
2. $10
3. no
4. Answers will vary.

page 26
1. D 5. A
2. B 6. H
3. E 7. F
4. G 8. C

page 27
1. cow—dairy—ice cream
2. tomatoes—cannery—pizza parlor
3. sheep—loom & spinning wheel—hat & gloves
4. trees—lumberyard—house
5. apples—bakery—apple pie

pages 28-29
Check map to see that student has written names of missing states:
Alaska, Arizona, Arkansas, Alabama, Florida, Oregon, Oklahoma, Ohio, Tennessee, Texas
1. Answers will vary. Check map for accuracy.
2. Check map to see that student has located cities correctly.
3. Answers will vary. Check map for accuracy.
4. Hawaii
5. Answers will vary. Check map for accuracy.

pages 30-31
1. Colorado
2. Connecticut
3. Indiana
4. Kansas
5. Nevada
6. Maine
7. North Carolina
8. New York
9. New Jersey
10. Hawaii

page 32
1. willow ptarmigan
2. forget-me-not
3. Sitka spruce
4. Juneau
5. Yukon River
6. Mt. McKinley
7. Barrow
8. Fairbanks
9. Alaska
10. Aleutian

page 33
Answers will vary.
Check for accuracy.

pages 34-35
Check to see that student draws a route that goes to each country listed in 1–19. The party is in Puerto Rico!

page 36
1. mountain
2. valley
3. plateau
4. river
5. lake
6. bay
7. peninsula
8. island
9. beach
10. plain
11. ocean

page 37
Eastern Hemisphere:
    Africa, Asia, Europe, Australia, Antarctica
Southern Hemisphere:
    South America, Africa, Australia, Asia, Antarctica
Western Hemisphere:
    North America, South America, Antarctica, Asia
Northern Hemisphere:
North America, South America, Europe, Asia, Africa

page 38
1. c
2. a
3. b
4. c
5. b
6. b
7. c
8. c
9. a
10. b
11. c
12. b

page 39
Cities (green):
Chicago, London, Moscow, Mexico City, Tokyo

States (blue):
Kansas, Vermont, Florida, Arizona, Hawaii, Texas

Countries (red):
Brazil, Egypt, Israel, Spain, India, Korea

Continents (yellow):
Asia, Antarctica, Europe, South America, Africa

pages 40–41
Check to see that student has accurately labeled continents.

Check to see that student has drawn a line from each child to the approximate location of the country.

pages 42–43
1. B
2. F
3. D
4. A
5. C
6. E
7. J
8. K
9. H
10. I
11. G
12. L

page 44
Answers will vary. Check to see that answers are correct.

page 45
1. A, 3
2. D, 1
3. D, 2
4. C, 1
5. A, 4
6. B, 1
7. A, 1
8. B, 2
9. D, 4
10. C, 3
11. B, 4
12. C, 4

pages 46–47
Answers will vary.

page 48
Check to see that flags are colored accurately.

7 red stripes
6 white stripes
13 stars

7 red stripes
6 white stripes
50 stars

page 49
1. c
2. b
3. b
4. b
5. c
6. c
7. a

page 50
1. 100
2. the first railroad
3. yes
4. 1927
5. yes
6. yes
7. 1869
8. Armstrong

page 51
Answers will vary.

page 52
A. 4
B. 5
C. 3
D. 9
E. 8
F. 2
G. 6
H. 10
I. 1
J. 7

page 53
Answers will vary.

pages 54–55
1. Pennsylvania Avenue
2. Pennsylvania Avenue
3. a and c
4. a and b
5. b and c
6. Constitution
7. Independence
8. Answers will vary.

page 56
1. Scotland
2. Italy
3. England
4. Belgium
5. Ireland
6. Wales
7. Norway
8. Germany

page 57
1. Chicago
2. New York
3. $1\frac{1}{2}$ million
4. $3\frac{1}{2}$ million
5. San Diego
6. Houston
7. $7\frac{1}{2}$ million
Answers will vary.

Copyright ©1998 by Incentive Publications, Inc., Nashville, TN.

Basic Skills/Social Studies 2-3